Table Of Contents

Seraphim On Cusp Of Spring

She passed me in the darkness with a smile
On the cold last night of winter that made
Me desire to hold her in my embracing arms
And feel the warmth of amour as the spring
Banishes deep frigid snow wind and showers
Even as she strolled away from me an angel
Whose beauty was divinely conceived by God
To whom nightly I raise prayers for a wife
To fill in the missing pieces of my puzzle
Of solitude under the light moon and stars
Of unfulfilled longing shining bright over
The sacred river I cross for a cup of java
At The Holy City diner where I pass nights
Of loneliness pondering my single state as
Hours fly while I replay in bachelor brain
All the lovely women it's been a privilege
To view through the eyes of a loving mind.

The Decision To Pursue Normalcy

Few realize the monumentality of my job
To stay sane and sober for hard reality
Of crazy drunks and glassy-eyed addicts
Staring into void of finite destruction
By self-medication to feel mad delusion
Of invincibility while in fact impotent
To change the intensity of their habits
Even as war violence and chaos encircle
This globe so Nature turns its terrible
Wrath against both guilty and innocents
Bawling at the iniquities to which they
Are subjected where the sun shines cold
Leading to a winter of great discontent
And Lord appears more distant than ever
Reluctant to come to save psycho planet
Of wondrous beauty and infinite variety
Of life that encompasses all this world
When peoples are just one single factor
As we spin through grandeur of universe
Which seems not to care about the Earth
Sum total of what mankind can perceive.

Reflection Upon Being An Artist

Having dedicated a quarter-century
To the craft of my poetry I intuit
That I have finally hit the stride
I have long sought through ages of
Solitude with my typewriter typing
The days and ways of this lifetime
Soaring with the speed of a bullet
Aimed at heart and mind integrated
In my body longing for a true love
Who shall be able to help me write
Some verses that will relieve agony
Of aloneness I have endured to see
A happiness I know is possible but
As of now unrealized creating poem
Which will adorn my gravestone for
The eternity on which I am focused
While I pass life single conjuring
Images to survive the test of time
In the view of critics and readers
I hope will find solace at the end
Of the entire oeuvre I've composed
In the course of this existence as
I try to impress my perfect woman.

Awaiting A True God Dale

I want to wage noble fight

To be worthy in Lord's sight

Who represents all power and might

In Whose eyes humans are slight

Causing us to cower in fright

When He appears on fated night

Blinding all with an omnipotent light

So to judge corrupt and right

Who won't feel fiery lake's bite

While evil ones land in hell

No longer able lies to tell

As all people hear ominous bell

Not heard since first man fell

Thrown from Eden with sorrowful yell

At last sentenced to Earthly cell

Where little seems to go well

Trying pain of sin to quell

And Paradise once again does jell.

Dale History As A Poet

Having honor to meet Ogden Nash

Who transformed humorous verse into cash

Though I was just youngster brash

Until into psychosis I did crash

When illness did my reality smash

Making normal life turn to ash

As fellow patients delusions did bash

While nightly I drank southern sourmash

So six years passed in flash

Finally arriving at the bachelor's pad

Fighting hard emotions making me sad

Deep enough to think myself mad

Haunted by ideas I was bad

Rarely finding reasons to be glad

And not realizing potential I had

To be more than poetic fad

Becoming to my works adoring dad

Whereupon I succeeded as college grad.

The Power Of The Lyric

Every poem unfolds with inner logic

That in great ones is magic

Whether due to rhythm or rhyme

It exists in a weightless time

Creating for audience a fiery light

Growing from some vital personal insight

Into the machinations of human life

Even if filled with complex strife

While it gives the reader pleasure

In a manner hard to measure

Though the words make small treasure

That comes from a simple verse

Which reverses stigma of evil curse

Of ignorance to beauty of existence

Through ideas whose combination is intense

Helping to make its listeners see

Creative strength arising from the free

Expression of sentiments leading to love

The only emotion sent from above

By Lord Who in Heaven reigns

Well aware of all petty pains.

Portrait Of An Adult Artist

To integrate the sacred and profane

In a language complex but plain

Is my most primary poetic aim

By which I'll make my name

Staying sane sober concrete and straight

In order to fulfill predestined Fate

Making Heaven on Earth the goal

Thus to save my fragile soul

Until I hear the celestial choir

And avoid terrible lake of fire

While I seek heir to sire

As the years fade into decades

Pursuing the quest for marrying maids

With whom to pass the time

In which lust is no crime

Through this life happy and long

Loving Muse who sings her song

Whom I dearly want to hold

When I grow gray and old

And we appear upon divine stage

So to leave behind troubled age.

Form Does Indeed Dictate Content

I'm not one to be cynical

Although I have often been skeptical

Especially when The Holiest City Oracle

Told me to expect divine miracle

That will drive most people hysterical

Because world's end is as comical

And entertaining as any Broadway musical

In manner that is not rabbinical

When Lord's cycle comes full circle

So we see whom to bury

Along with woman I will marry

If I survive end times scary

Saved by Tinkerbell silent Disney fairy

Destined happily wondrous news to carry

To the Great Queen Mother Mary

Betrothed to The Good Judge Larry

While on the planet we tarry

Executing against death a perfect parry.

Brief Summary Of An Autobiography

It's time to put away fears
And turn my back on tears
Because I've had home thirty years
No longer seeking solace of beers
While family has been truly dears
As specter of age sixty nears
While my desire for fame steers
Where I read poems to peers
And endless day into decades disappears
As masterpieces I try to write
Before my eyes lose my sight
Until I'm overwhelmed by divine light
Putting up a last-ditch fight
To enunciate all that is right
About kingdom of Lord's infinite might
In Whose view I'm individual slight
Though thinking myself with Him tight
Through cold dawn into frigid night.

Paean To Most Lovely Muse

You are as fragile precious and beautiful
As a pair of frail butterfly wings riding
Wind of South American hill causing storm
On the shores of Gulf of Mexico even when
The sun shines bright down on New Orleans
As I ponder grace of your love reflecting
Lights into eyes of Deity watching planet
Made wondrous by your sweet presence full
Of the hope for salvation transforming an
Apathetic existence into life of meaning.

I Am Only A Poet

Only a poet can compose in words a portrait of the beauty

You create by your presence in the world

Only a poet can immortalize the bounty of the goodness

You represent by the bliss of your body

Only a poet can capture in verse the sacred grace

You exude through the magic of the air

Only a poet can rhapsodize the intricacies of your cosmic

Dance upon the stage of universal knowing

Only a poet can cherish with passion the poetess you became

By overcoming the agonies of Earthly reality

Only a poet can edify the cathedral of your intensity

With sentiments of longing that knows no end

Only a poet can describe the essence of your perfection

In the mind of an audience seeking lost meanings

Only a poet can compete with The Lord for the saving spirit

Of this globe He left in a far distant past

Only a poet can express the craving for salvation every person

Feels but no other may with skill enunciate

Only a Poet can love you.

But You Alone Are Queen

The breath of the bust the beauty of the body
The Velvet of the voice the ideal of the eyes
The spark of the smile the length of the legs
The feature of the face the lilt of the laugh
The mystery of the mind the wisp of the waist
Inspire this artist to great work of Creation
But every man can pursue only one unique Muse
As solitary visions roam over landscapes full
Of past temptations that have no more meaning
Except in their absence while gladly embraced
The rest of the planet vanishes into shade of
Indescribably sensual union beyond any poetic
Expressions inadequate to convey the emotions
Of the grace of your divine reality in world.

Passionate Obsession Isn't Politically Correct

True Romance is not wimpy vague or indecisive
And thus is out-of-step with very ambiguities
That have come to typify not only these times
But also the craft of poetry that now has met
Its tragic Fate of sad irrelevance as writers
No longer express intense longings of mankind
But rather waffle about gardening and reality
As something impotent and harmless when daily
Millions are touched by the ravages of hunger
Disease and genocide which only Love conquers
Even as it is treated as cotton-candy emotion
Tasty for a few minutes but without substance
A perception not just false but dangerous for
Every human who tries to comprehend this life
As an ambivalent gift full of tragedy as well
As bliss achieved solely by a strong devotion
To ideal visions ever fewer people can grasp.

Reflection On The Eternal Obsession

Females are hot springs of geyser emotions
Erupting with a periodic regularity of mad
Kinetic energy creating desires for unions
Of lust and love devotion and passion want
And fulfillment as the planet continues to
Sustain both deep and petty feelings while
People wrestle with the whims of a Reality
Of longing for the divine bliss of a grace
Granted by a benevolent Lord hidden by the
Illusions of time and space unfolding sure
Of amorous consummations pulling lovers to
The sweet satisfaction of unending kisses.

The Origin Of My Uniqueness

When The Lord told me to be God
I followed His order without compunction
Doing the job the best way I could conceive
Accepting my Fate and being ready to die
To further the idea of a worldly illumination
By ingesting as many substances as I could
Until I was detained for suffering an illness
By authorities unable to comprehend a reality
Based upon a personal divinity I couldn't deny
To the shrinks who interrogated me with desire
To save me from the abyss into which I dove
Fully conscious of the consequences of my actions
Going with the inarguable flow of a raging river
Heading to the falls of a supernatural insight
Tumbling down the mountain of the sacred presence
In Whom I trusted while society labeled me insane
And I was subjected to the necessity of medicines
Sedating me from completing the holy mission
To which I honestly felt the Deity had called me
If I hoped to achieve salvation for this mad planet.

Fairest And Sweetest Of Hearts

When I am frustrated at your democratic treatment of your friends

I must remember that is the reason I love you

When I get upset when you show weakness in your resolutions

I must remember your humanity is your greatest trait

When I await your telephone calls so seconds seem like hours

I must remember you have your own life to live

When I feel jealous you spend time with other companions

I must remember I just recently entered your sphere

When I imagine you are being frivolous and evasive towards me

I must remember I have my own issues of denial

When I desire madly to monopolize the gift of your enthusiasm

I must remember the Lord created you to brighten the world

When I find fault with you for mistakes everybody must make

I must remember Jesus Christ was the sole perfect being

When I dream of you with longing in the silence of the night

I must remember my prayers for guidance with you

When the days appear grave and bleak without your presence

I must remember you also experience dark times

And when you tell me I am your best friend and fantastic buddy

I remember until I met you I was alone and bitter

But now am filled with hope where there once was despair

And bliss where there was tragedy I have overcome

With the strength of the self-worth you have bestowed on me

When with your perfect brown eyes and lipstick smile

You blessed me with perpetual sunshine of your humor

Transporting me to summit of ecstasy from which I can view

The spectacular vista of the possibility for true happiness.

A Fool Only In Love

You short-circuit my brain
With craving to be in your presence
My vaunted intellect cannot control
As great hormones of early spring kick in
And I sit fixated by the silent telephone
Waiting for the ring of your Velour voice
Lost in long moments of amorous oblivion
While I read the Bible to increase faith
In Lord Who directed you into my reality
Formerly resigned to indifferent solitude
Until special day in pub you materialized
To create in my sad existence new meaning
Even as you melted my defenses with torch
Of the kindness concern and interest
By which you illuminated my darkness
As I recited to you the poems inspired
By the purity of your essential beauty
Which thunder struck me with a longing
I had not experienced for score of years
So I fell into an adolescent infatuation
That continues to grow into deep infatuation
Transforming my aloneness into a sentiment
Of wholeness I never thought I could feel.

Some Days Tougher Than Others

At times when I am bent under the weight of my universe

I will remember your exuberance

At times when I feel overwhelmed by my situation

I will recall your happy enthusiasm

At times when I worry needlessly about your behavior

I will remind myself of your resilience

At times when I fear my demons will devour me

I will find solace in your perseverance

At times when the world seems hopeless and depressed

I will be comforted by your vivacity

At times when I crave to make our relationship carefree

I will cherish your unending friendship

At times when I start unfairly to judge your escapades

I will adore the gift of your humanity

At times when daily reality appears harsh and cruel

I will treasure your sacred presence

At times when I find it hard to keep a smile on my face

I will be made joyful by your vitality

And if at any time I fail to appreciate your complexities

I will beg you to forgive my myopia

For I love you as a precious diamond among coal of Earth

In whose reflections I see my own weaknesses

Made trivial by the light of your brilliance.

The Hard Process Of Reality

I often feel a great pain
At loss of Remo and Shane
Buddies prematurely taken from this life
Who both left behind grieving wife
And knew me before reclaiming sanity
When I filled myself with vanity
Of being the only true God
As blasphemous path I blithely trod
Convinced we would all live forever
And nothing on Earth could sever
The ties that hold us here
Because death caused me no fear
Feeling heaven to be quite near
Though now I see my mistake
No longer prone to psychotic break
Even as I mourn departed friends
Trying with Lord to make amends
For hubris of my divine delusions
Seeking to get beyond evil illusions
Of powers I thought I possessed
When with divinity I was obsessed.

Photos Don't Dew You Justice

With two roses I seek to win your heart

The pink reflecting beauty of your face

And the red symbolic of devoted passion

You cause me to feel carousing in amour

As the hours disappear into fine memory

Of the brief time we've shared in world

Of temporary liaisons and lost romances

Even as we build a citadel of certainty

That will not vanish as long as we stay

Together in the brown clairvoyant sight

Of your eyes enticing me to reveries of

Future fulfillment we both will cherish

Strolling in bliss down blessed avenues

Of a mutual knowledge that solitary God

Allows us to celebrate every night love

Blooms in the garden of separate bodies

United by the desire for a consummation

That can survive the many obstacles our

Longing for the other makes irrelevant.

A True Heart Dale Celebration

You have given me dear Elizabeth

A reason for my every breath

For you're sexy smart and fine

And agreed to be my Valentine

Which I take as a positive sign

I can exist with realistic hope

With you passion I can scope

Because just in nick of time

You gave meaning to my rhyme

To seek reality sober and straight

So need for intoxicants did abate

When each other we did meet

To pursue a great romantic feat

That led me to amorous bliss

Even if we've yet to kiss

For I cherish everything about you

Which keeps me from becoming blue

About the problems in my life

That once caused me deep strife

But you've set my spirit free

By your loving concern for me.

Watch What You Ask For

Two weeks after telling me he didn't want
To grow old my friend Bob got off his bus
In Hoboken and dropped dead at sixty when
Most people begin to feel pull of old age
And every night I ask God to direct me in
My relationship with Muse I think I adore
Even as I consider the sticks of dynamite
Of illness age and philosophy differences
That will be ready to destroy foundations
Of any interaction we might enjoy so that
We must continually co-exist under strain
Of pressures it will be tough to overcome
Despite fact that there seems a potential
For a true and lasting affair between our
Mutual desires and reality of our craving
For a common devotion making us both glad
God has grandly brought us to each other.

Spring Arrives Just One Annually

Winter died with a thirty-minute blizzard
I missed this morning dreaming about Muse
I fear fears to be alone with me although
I surely realize she can trust me even as
I watch the vernal equinox with high hope
Deity shall bless any future romance with
Intensity as being able to say I Love You
Whenever we part is rush greater than any
I ever felt under influence of intoxicant
Substances I have outgrown like delusions
Of perfection I perceive now aren't found
On this accidental planet where I attempt
To grow with the blossoms on nude trees I
View in pursuit of true amour calling all
To insights of bliss every person desires
In broken world but in fact only The Lord
Can experience safe in mansion of Heaven.

Those Who Would Be Wordsmiths

Clarity is the refuge of verbal technicians
Who regard verse as an engineering exercise
While craftsmen find amusement in the plays
Between words rolled like dice across pages
Of vocabulary gambles filled with a meaning
By which is sometimes won critical approval
But the poet writes in images a paradoxical
Tension in which the only certainty is true
Uncertainty of reality morphing like mobius
Strip into different perspective reconciled
Only in the internal logic of the opus full
Of an ambiguity describing lucid insight of
Creative mind struggling to comprehend real
Essence of life on this sadly confused spot
To which all creatures have been condemned.

Living In A Mythical Past

I am Achilles come back to claim the long life

Lost at Troy when I was struck by Apollo arrow

And descended to the Lordship of an underworld

From which it seemed I would never more escape

Until I became aware of the intense loveliness

Of Eris presence in the world where I returned

Full of a great longing for a sensuous passion

Which sustained me through decades of solitude

Even as I spent the years in dedicated studies

Of the ways one can adore his reasons for joy.

To Inaugurate Festival Of Eris

Great Goddess of Discord Chaos and Trouble

You are the fairest of all Olympic deities

After Whom Zeus lusted with supreme desire

And for Whom the gold apple was fabricated

Which led to an immature judgment by Paris

Resulting in death of noble Greek Achilles

Who came back after three Hadean millennia

Even as Yahweh used your fruit to test Eve

And Adam who couldn't handle divine beauty

By which You sustain spirit of underworld.

The Subtle Paradox Of Language

My poetry treads the tricky tightrope
Strung over gap between love and lust
Passion and porno liberty and license
Even while it digresses to reflection
On the essence of carnal knowledge in
The real world where it is ignored as
The vast majority of possible readers
Go about their daily routine unaware
That I exist much less caring about a
Wordsmith hidden in The Holiest City.

The Source Of My Prolificacy

I have Muse happy to be inspiration
Even though from younger generation
Who excites me by her subtle beauty
Which I believe it is my great duty
To describe in verses which I share
With rest of the world sad but fair
Because it has lost ability to love
Cut off from presence of Lord above
Since Eve's expulsion from Paradise
When He decided to stop being nice.

When God Comes To Visit

I dream of conjugal contortions

On the bed of pure consummation

Reflecting glory of Lord seeing

The intensity of our dedication

To the happiness of the other's

Longing for grace justification

In the arms of a holy salvation

Even as years fly like swallows

In the atmosphere of the desire

To be worthy of Deity presence.

Let Fate Follow Its Destiny

If you are the lady from the future I think you are

Then nothing I Dew will change the path of journeys

On which together we will embark and if you are not

Who I think you are you have still put a fire under

My frozen heart to show me the possibilities I feel

Have become manifest for some type of true love for

You have filled my spirit with a hope of finding an

Amour with whom I can spend the rest of the earthly

Time I have before my descent into the silent grave

That pulls us all into an oblivion of mortal sleep.

Now That I've Found You

I have always wanted you badly

Just wishing to kiss you madly

And you are my sacred star

So I no longer need bar

For you to illuminate my mind

Having to other females become blind

Full of longing for your smile

You deliver with inimitable style

As we travel many a mile

In your hot silver sports auto

Growing in love with the flow

Of the great river of desire

As we're filled with amorous fire

Trying to the other to devote

The hours of legends we wrote

When we spoke of dedicated love

As you wore sacred Velvet glove

In the reality of ages past

When passion between us did last

Swimming the abyss of great ocean

As creatures of deep eternal emotion.

Ideation Of Being In Love

I want to hold you kiss you and embrace simultaneously

I want to stun you with the insight of my intelligence

I want to have healthy liaison without self-medication

I want to be intimate with longing body and clear mind

I want to hug you on the beach of your island paradise

I want to converse with you until the death of the sun

I want to grab you with the strength of my loving arms

I want to read you all the poetry you can ever inspire

I want to adore you with every resource of happy heart

I want to fill you with an amorous desire to be my gal

I want you to be the woman to whom to dedicate my soul

I want you to seek the same things as strongly as I do

I want us to find Romance many people think impossible

In these times in which the Apocalypse seems imminent.

One and Only Magnificent Muse

I express my passion through my poetic art

Rather than in everyday routine of Reality

For I don't want to possess or control you

Emotionally because I want us to grow into

A mutual bloom of love which knows no true

Domination as communication's possible for

Equals alone talking in tones of actuality

Leading to fulfillment and laughter as our

Minutes together spiral into soft embraces

Of common respect for sacred relationship.

Muse Happy With Her Position

In a life defined by vital milestones

Meeting you might be the seminal fact

By which true meaning can be found as

I dedicate myself to creation of poem

Which will be considered truly unique

Like the harmony of the melody of the

Symphony of your smile and the beauty

Of your body calling me to deep ideas

Of satisfaction in your love embraces

Pulling me away from era of solitude.

My Lady From The Future

Like the Missouri into the Mississippi

Flows our destiny into each other from

Separate streams while under the still

Surface roil tidal waves of an anxiety

About distinction between friendliness

And Romance longing to swim in current

Of your kisses as I ponder integrities

Of our different perspectives by which

We define ourselves trying to see love

Merging together in our trip to ocean.

The Paradox Of The Wordsmith

The greater the fame of the poet

The more likely negative critics

Will condemn his creative oeuvre

For literary approval is quality

Rarely handed to inspired living

Versifiers trying to get a break

By which their opus will be read

By a public apathetic to efforts

To create verbal meaning in work

Which is real to the uninformed.

Reflection On Your Unique Personality

You might not be the prettiest peacock in this theme park

But my poetic creativity flies on the wing of your beauty

And you might not be truly the sharpest pencil in the box

But my inspirations are guided by light of your intellect

And you might not have the most buxom body on sandy beach

But my libido longs to gaze upon you in a tropical bikini

And you might not be most sacred saint the world has seen

But my heart beats to the musical rhythm of your kindness

And you might not be as fulfilled as you would like to be

But my bliss is founded upon cornerstone of your presence

And you might not be able to avoid madness of your dreams

But my prayers every hour are dedicated to your happiness

And though we might never be the joyful couple I hope for

Still your friendship is holiest reward Lord has bestowed

On any male who has ever experienced the human condition.

In Sonnet A Perfect Form

If you're my wife it's written in the stars
Far from planet of reactors and cars
Where men pristine rivers daily pollute
And criminals without discretion shoot
Innocent folk who cannot safely hide
From the barrel of mortality's gun
But if you turn out to be my sole Bride
I will live forever in light of sun
Of radiant brilliance of your beauty
Which makes me want to compose sacred verse
To neutralize solitudinous curse
I must overcome as a creative duty
To immortalize your porcelain face
Filling all who see it with sublime grace.

Why We Still Stick Together

I am older than you by nineteen years

Raising specter of April-October romance

And over past loves we've shed many tears

But between us there is definite chance

We could become truly passionate pair

As I find you indescribably fair

While you're attracted to the intellect

Which allows me to speak what is correct

When I consider beauty of amour

I feel whenever I'm in your presence

For you cause everything to make sense

By loveliness I've never seen before

Since time I moved into bachelor's pad

And with you in my life I'm always glad.

My Love Affaire With Emily

We are both poets who lived as recluses
Myself in Hackensack she in Amherst
For our styles we never made excuses
Though on the writers' scene we did not burst
But she composed with images obscure
While I prefer concepts concrete and sure
Inspired by objects like cigarette ashes
As she found meaning in clever dashes
She employed to emphasize her off-beat rhymes
For which she has been mentor to me
As I explored potential of verse free
So I emulated her many times
When I sought to describe something just right
Because she's my perfect poetic light.

Cocktail Waitress Working Punk Club

She had precisely proportioned amount
Of lovely chest flesh and a perfectly
Formed hour-glass figure pouring into
Stash of ass too hot to smoke covered
By a tattered skirt revealing sensual
Fishnet marble of lithe chiseled legs
With grin to spark black fire of hell
Strolling through enthusiastic masses
Of appreciative drunks imbibing shots
In a distinctive hurry to permit them
To grab her attention for more rounds
While I admired hard svelte gyrations
She executed in her dutiful movements
Past tables packed with empty bottles
Unable to screw up the courage to ask
Her for anything but another icy shot
Dreaming of a liaison with an urgency
Of the manic music inducing wild kids
To mosh their bodies on a dance floor
Where she is a true luxuriant skater.

Waiting To Get Java Refill

Lovely waitress at diner is angel

In body face and voice justifying

High prices for burgers and stack

Of pancakes delicious with butter

As the boss cashier reads a paper

And an occasional customer laughs

Through the well-lit emptiness of

Lost haven to which I retreat for

The consolations of companionship

When I crave to view vivid beauty

Of the server I desire like a cup

Of coffee energizing the midnight

With longing in a distant reality

Created by grace of fine presence

Of her for whom moon always glows

Through unending cycle of seasons

Reminding all of brevity of life.

Truly Getting To Know You

Just because I want to give you space
Doesn't mean I desire to see you less
To dedicate myself to actual intimacy
While we learn each other's quirks as
We meet in a present where the future
And past merge into midnight embraces
Full of happiness of a mutual passion
Under the dome of the great Milky Way
Looking down on the bliss sparking us
To experience reality of fulfillment.

Never Too Late For Amour

You reawakened love passion and devotion
In this ancient soul who has existed too
Long without the consolation of a friend
And companion to whom to dedicate spirit
Of creativity you bring out as I reflect
The beauty of sublime light you produced
In bitter darkness of my aloneness while
I labored to write poetry to fill a void
Of despair I felt for many years even as
I awaited your appearance in my reality.

This Life Is Too Easy

Mine is a spontaneous outpouring of enthusiasm

For the bliss of vitality of this earthly life

Reflecting the beauty of Lord's grace covering

The mattress of humanity with a down comforter

Of insight into the machinations of big cosmos

Where everything is possible but nothing comes

Of value without a struggle in the psyche of a

Beholder of reality seeking to create order in

The chaos of the infinity of the Universe that

Spins like the wheel of galaxy where we exist.

When You Enter My thoughts

The choice is simple: give up my wastrel ways

Or risk absolute rejection by the only female

Who will ever ultimately matter to me while I

Pursue vitality in this myopic existence when

The years slide like waves upon the sand into

The ocean of precarious life which guarantees

Nothing but the sunrise at dawn and sunset at

Dusk pulling us into the mystery of shy night

As the stars show themselves in subtly modest

Lights of insight into the workings of world.

My Flame Once Again Ignited

Indescribable are the depths of my love for you

As I swim trying not to drown in sea of emotion

Circling like a shark around the lifeboat of my

Longing for the sweet liquor of truly beautiful

Smile of your body infusing my soul with desire

For an intimacy it seems at times we will never

Enjoy as you entice your myriad suitors to idea

Of consummate fulfillment with your secret kiss

Overwhelming heavens with a scent of perfection

From stimulating perfume of your presence which

Calls me to a contemplation of the ideal female

You represent from the burst of dawn to scarlet

Of dusk pulling us into another night apart for

The sake of sanity because passion truly drives

The chemicals of my brain into configuration of

Madness I can barely control when I regard holy

Visage with which you bless sober path creating

The sanctity of a cathedral to my straight mind

Reflecting the wishes of a generation of lovers

Forever dedicated to concrete myths of Romance.

Birthday Greetings To Best Friend

You've always had a golden heart

Which has translated into unique art

In both painting and perfect verse

Even as you battle against curse

Of women you love who shun

The brilliance of your human sun

By which their senses you stun

By the intensity of your love

As pure as eyes of dove

Lovely as any picture you paint

Being close to being actual saint

You are better than human race

Or any other beings in space

For you are blessed by Lord

And by many unknown admirers adored

As you always wage good fight

To be holy in divine sight

Hoping to find an ideal mate

And arrive finally at happy Fate

Where you meet your perfect Bride

Who'll forever be by your side.

Yet Another Great Evening Together

You are more fluent in the language of Romance

Than I could ever hope to be despite my verses

Created during dearth of true relationships as

The decades have passed waiting for sentiments

Of passion and desire to find the proper woman

To drag me away from the aloofness that I long

To escape even as the season calls all to hold

Lovers in warm embraces under wool blankets so

The atmosphere of dark cold nights is made hot

By the intensity of the amour that they share.

Farewell To Dewster Heavenly Mansion

No matter how much I crave to smother you in the embrace

Of my hungry arms I shall not compromise true principles

I hold as gentleman and buddy not to force myself on you

And love you in every way possible looking at the desire

I experience when I breathe the intoxicant aroma of your

Presence filling me with ever deeper appreciation of the

Secret narcotic of the female appeal calling all men for

The brief moment of Eternity to consider real deficiency

Of the absurdity of an existence spent in hot pursuit of

Material luxuries that are ultimately of picayune value.

Dealing With Addiction To Muse

Objections abound about the voluminosity

Of works where I describe her luminosity

But lady is for me a benevolent narcotic

Who has kept me from being mad psychotic

Though I've done with her nothing erotic

Despite my feelings she may be true love

Even as I seek to wear fine Velvet glove

Ready to devote myself to future unclear

If only I could lovely voice always hear

Passing through days running into decade

In which she would consent to be my maid

So that we could experience mutual bliss

With me as her man and she as happy miss

Content to dedicate her brief Earth time

To being the reason behind my glad rhyme

Thus to lose our senses in great embrace

To demonstrate potential of peoples race

And if I am overcome by a gigantic amour

I apologize for being real literary bore

But I must write what the heart composes

For she is to my spirit a vine of roses.

Everything About You Is Heaven

When I broke up with I-want-to-get-married-because-my-
Biological-clock-is-expiring-and-I-wish-to-bear-a-kid-
Before-it's-too-late-despite-meeting-at-insane-asylum-
So-the-chances-are-high-our-children-would-inherit-an-
Insidious-illness-I-shall-never-pass-on-to-only-scion-
I-might-ever-father-last-girlfriend eighteen years ago
I realized I'd probably die an avuncular bachelor when
I comprehended I was condemning myself to a cruel life
Of solitude and poetic isolation without a Muse before
I found you to make irrelevant the era of my aloneness
As you re-ignited the furnace of my amorous longing in
The somber shadows of my heart full with determination
To be worthy of your friendship and compassion even if
We never consummate for your soul is the star of grace
I felt had vanished from the Milky Way sky under which
I pray the two of us have felt a joy meaning and truth
Able to survive many obstacles to glad days of Romance
We've uncovered for each other while love hours tumble
Into a future when we could forever dedicate ourselves
To intensive passion upon which holy God can look down
From the blessed mansion where we're eternal roommates
To sanctify the devotion our relationship exemplifies.

The Prayer Of A Wordsmith

Great Lord Above please look down
On my literary works and bless me
With great patience of a novelist
To describe with words situations
That resonate with an audience as
They follow flow of the narrative
And grant me clear precision of a
Poet to express universal thought
While giving me the fine insights
Of an essayist knowledgeable in a
Subject about which one craves to
Know the essence while filling me
With real ability of a playwright
To resolve the conflict of dramas
Upon which all literature's based
As I employ the creativity that's
The foundation of all I composed.

What It Means Being Dale

It is not at the moment of passionate climax
But rather at the quiet minute of daily life
When lovers have nothing to say but converse
To get to know each other more deeply that a
True love shows its anxious visage like babe
Crying denied its mother's fine milk flowing
Like river rapids over mountain rocks hiding
From the desires of currents carrying salmon
To spawning spots trying to avoid bear claws
Even as the soft seduction of sunlight sends
Embraced partners to the abyss of loneliness
Wherein is found the sweet tonic of solitude
Calling all creatures to reflection on death
Rendered impotent by great promises of grace
By which all are forgiven their earthly sins
While seeking the immortal salvation of Lord
Able to snatch us from the world at any time
No matter how great our attachment to globe.

The Foundation Of My Devotion

It is remotely possible someone loves you more than I

But nobody you will ever encounter believes in you as I Dew

Because I believe you have the purest heart yet conceived

Because I believe you have a genuine desire to be well

Because I believe you can control designs of your demons

Because I believe you embody a Spirit that is invincible

Because I believe you carry a capacity for love that is endless

Because I believe you are strong enough to conquer your problems

Because I believe you try to shelter loved ones from your pain

Because I believe you always act in ways to make things right

Because I believe you have empathy for every person you meet

Because I believe you exercise will to uncover hard answers

Because I believe you possess the determination to triumph

Because I believe you will allow nothing to stop your happiness

Because I believe you represent divine Reality of salvation

Because I believe you are a living example of God's grace

Because I believe in overwhelming intelligence of your soul

Because I have experienced divinity of your Earthly passion

Showing me the sacred actuality of potential of this life

Growing in beauty every day by the light of your brilliance.

Muse Not Just For Me

I must realize you produce feelings
Of desire and longing in every male
You know that are as strong as mine
Even as I oftentimes believe lovely
Verse you inspire me to conceive is
Distraction to expression of actual
Sentiments I should not hide in the
Maze of words that disguise my true
Craving I carry to hold you forever
In loving bear hug of deep embrace.

Muse For Entire Male Race

Thank you for allowing me the privilege
Of ending every meeting by "I Love You"
Even as you deal with psychos desperate
To claim you exclusively for themselves
When you are in fact God's gift to life
While I hover in this solo apartment as
The hours of solitude are reinforced by
Velvet perfection of your concern about
The welfare of my spirit longing to hug
You through the insanity of Apocalypse.

Krakatoa Of My Lusting Spirit

The magma of my desire builds with pressure

Beneath the cone of the volcano of my longing

Thought extinct despite the plumes of sulphur

Escaping into the atmosphere of my cravings

To caress your perfect form with infernal heat

Of lava pouring down the mountain canyons

Of my wish for endless consummation exploding

In a blast which shall be forever remembered

By skeptics who underestimated the intensity

Of the burning ardor I experience for you

Without violating the limits of attraction

We both respect in effort to tame emotions

That could create a tsunami of fulfillment

Beneath the vast trenches of the Pacific abyss

Destabilized by possibility of volatile climax

Likely to drown islands of aquatic insecurity

From which masses of terrified humanity flee

As we oblivious lose our senses to an after-life

Of immortal lip-lock from which only Armageddon

Can tear us asunder reinforced by devoted will

To unite in passion through the cosmic nano-second

Of Eternity.

The Bridge To Midnight Java

I walk under full rainbow halo moon

And ponder essence of color and light

While in my head plays a romantic tune

Filled with wonder at miracle of sight

Letting me view my only chosen girl

As precious as large perfectly formed pearl

Retrieved from the bottom of vast ocean

Who infects me with amorous notion

That together we are destined to be

Finding happiness in mutual life

Even if we don't become man and wife

For we both want to live forever free

Which does not diminish truth of our love

Being brought to each other by Lord above.

What Use Is Great Poetry

It was chance that brought you into my life

Because you could have been anyone in world

But it is pre-destination that will keep us

Together for you are you the female I adore

And desire with a pure heart translating my

Craving sentiments into verses of a passion

Which knows neither the hard demise of time

Nor the sad consequences of a loss of amour

By which I fabricate poems to sanctify deep

Longing I feel when I hear your kind voice.

As Howl Freezing Winter Winds

Loving you has always been my goal

For I think you're my mate of soul

With whom I can pass my Earth time

While I devote my spirits to rhyme

In poems that with passion I write

Because you are divine in my sight

So in mad truly amorous hug I long

To compose with you lyrics to song

That will become a big rocking hit

For into puzzle of myself you fit.

Swimming In Ocean Of Muse

Since we met I have been wading over sandbars
Uncovered at low tide of desires and devotion
Walking ever deeper into water of your beauty
Until I must now decide whether to retrace my
Steps or plunge into dark depths where sharks
Threaten my safety as strong high tide washes
Me away from the solidity of white sand shore
Where my love sits under an umbrella awaiting
My return unaware of the dangers I experience
Trying to navigate the undertow of dedication
To the unknown you create by the perfection I
Perceive in the abyss of your lovely form and
The unfathomable profundity of the compassion
With which you feed the creatures of this sea
Wherein at times I desperately crave to drown
To awaken to an eternal embrace in your arms.

Not To Ignore The Physical

"Love ya'" echoes through my brain at the end

Of every conversation filling me with longing

For the tasty fruits of sweet sensuous favors

Even as I have been wary of forcing my desire

To the forefront of our relationship which is

One of two whole people not just the union of

Two minds though I adore your personality and

The joy of your Spirit but I can't deny wants

Of my body craving the fine consolation of an

Embrace with kisses uniting us into the bliss

Of mutual satisfaction by which to experience

A consummation to fulfill our unspoken dreams

Of happiness in shy loving arms of the other.

My Spirit Lost In Solitude

I do not want to spend the rest of my life

In regret I never gave Romance real chance

As I ponder love you've given me like I am

The brother you always lacked even as into

Passion for you I have fallen realizing it

An unlikely prospect but still I am filled

With carnal desires I cannot deny awaiting

The bliss of our lips joined in sweet kiss

It seems will not occur despite a devotion

To your happiness which I carry in my soul

Longing to hold you in a mutual embrace of

Pleasure growing from soil of a friendship

That is an acorn spouting into a great oak

In whose shade we can lounge together safe

From suitors unworthy of joy of our bliss.

Why Do We Question Destiny?

I don't truly believe in happily ever after

But I believe in you and I believe in myself

And I believe in us not necessarily as a romantic couple

But rather as a spiritual team fighting together

The evils of degeneracy addiction and drunken excess

From which we both are trying to escape with weapons

Of love grace patience laughter and redemption

Even as we maintain a respectful distance

From one another though we realize the potential for passion

That exists in our interactions full of devotion and longing

For an ideally unique consummation that might never happen

Despite the attraction we always feel in common presence

While we pass the years in an amorous oblivion

Preventing our lips from ever touching in an ardent kiss

Leading to an extraordinary union few humans can conceive

Lost in the pursuit of ephemeral possessions

Rather than in the search for an absolute love

Which is the only truly divine goal to be experienced

In the midst of the insanity of this crazy planet.

The Cold Season Of Devotion

I feel with my brain and think with my heart

But still I thrill to the dynamic tension

That exists between you and me given presence

Of Platonic love and the potential for physical

Passion between the reality of Romance

And the joyfulness of Friendship even as I long

To sweep you up into my arms and overwhelm you

With kisses to fill you with the craving for amour

With which you infect me when I admire the beauty

Of your svelte body desiring to hold you

In endless embrace transporting us to Paradise

Not experienced since fall of our first parents

From grace of the knowledge of divine Father

When by their disobedience was destroyed

The perfection of Eden to which I pray one day

Together we might be able in bliss to return.

Addiction Is A Possessive Mistress

Like a Chinese guard tower made of pure dew
About to disintegrate into cascade of tears
I struggle to find meaning in vast solitude
Rising like a tsunami from the roiling seas
Of possible intercourse with unknown ladies
Mocking me with an illusion of consummation
With their perfect bodies enticing me to dreams
Of unions never to be realized on the arid soil
Of this planet where I am condemned to solitary
Contemplation of amour I might find in embraces
Of ideal woman loving me despite idiosyncrasies
Caused by the infirmity created by an obsession
With whore of dissipation who sadly infected me
With contagious disdain for the happy pleasures
On which I turned my back long ago in the years
I spent in pursuit of shallow hedonistic utopia
I didn't understand could become veritable hell
Of divine delusions against which I truly fight
Trying to re-discover clarity of youthful brain
Destroyed in distant past by wish for false joy
Of life devoted to bliss of total intoxication.

Seeking Literati Who "Get" Me

My poetry unfurls with the crack of a bull-whip
Without punctuation without pause and without a
Regard for the niceties of the English language
Which is indeed a good tongue but I want to eat
The feast of tasty convention of literary mores
To fill the future with perspectives heretofore
Unknown because unseen in true canon of poetics
Touching the lace skirt of immortality while an
Appreciation of my vision blooms as a cactus in
The desert of current writings unable to attain
The lofty heights of former masters who changed
The landscape of literature by the chances took
When they planted small acorn of a literary oak
Still growing branches shading effort of superb
Wordsmiths doomed to accolades only after life.

Forecasting The Weather Of Devotion

Every heart is its own eco-system
Capable of going from blazing hot
To cyclonically chaotic with mere
Single word from the true beloved
Blotting out the sun like the orb
Of the moon in an eclipse even as
Desire incinerates the spirit for
The moments of lost amour felt in
The heat of infatuations by which
Every pure lover defines himself.

In Nighttime Reflections Of Sprummer

The half-moon hangs over the city
Like gargoyles from the height of
Notre Dame scoping Left Bank when
Artists and poets meet to discuss
Secrets of their respective craft
While drunks lose themselves to a
Reverie induced by the sweet wine
Of oblivion to the pain they feel
Pondering the intense meaning mad
Dissipation brings to their life.

Truly Simple Is Simply True

I love you

Like the diamond the light it refracts;

I adore you

Like an infant the comfort of a first teddy-bear;

I cherish you

Like the morning glory the sun that lets it bloom;

I treasure you

Like the hidden riches within the depths of the planet;

I want you

Like the air currents upon which winging swallows soar;

I need you

Like the oxygen that keeps alive every breathing creature;

I desire you

Like the delicious taste of a peach in perfect season;

I crave you

Like the fields of wheat the fertile soil where they grow;

I trust you

Like the innocent child the wisdom of deeply devoted parent;

And I respect you

Like the Great Judge the integrity of the correct rule of law

Because every morning I wake from a night of scattered dreams

To open my eyes once again to sweet sublime beauty of Reality

In which the gift of your fine presence fills me with longing

To hold you through the trials of doubt to which I am subject

Living a life where the actuality of the Lord is in question.

A First Intimation Of Falter

No moving objects disturb the peace of the sky
Except the moon reflecting the deep ocean blue
Of the night dome like the dash-board lighting
The face of a driver speeding to meet his love
Far away through the headlights of a sport car
Bought with the hard blood of his daily labors
As he ponders the luscious curves of his amour
And appeal of the perfect half-spheres of her ass
He craves to grab in his hands as minutes tick by
And the lunar orb journeys over highway he drives
With a magic found in her gazes whenever together
Even as the radio by design plays a favorite tune
He sings full of an anticipation of consummations
In the downy arms of sweet mistress fighting sigh
Of fulfillment while she's warmed by heat of lover
Till he rests in womb of her unforgetting passion.

Sonnet To Begin New Month

A brother needing sisters' affection

After trying for years to prove I'm God

As I sought impossible perfection

While in holy footsteps of Christ I trod

Though I have not died a horrific death

Begging for forgiveness with last breath

But divine delusions I have renounced

Since of psych unit's rubber walls I bounced

AS now I seek out Jesus' gift of Grace

To replace man's hatred with endless love

Hoping to wear my sole Bride's Velvet glove

Who truly has lovely but unknown face

I long voraciously to hold and kiss

Thus to be consumed by marital bliss.

Birthday Dale To Great Friend

You never came to Bachelor's Pad

But that doesn't make me sad

Since through times good and bad

We never at other got mad

While at your transformation I'm glad

Having given birth to super lad

Who every day grows a tad

And you adore truly his dad

Bucking the hard single parent fad

For you are true friend Trace

Who's finally found her sacred space

Getting to know meaning of Grace

As you adapt to new place

Where you hold a secret ace

While you adjust to the pace

Of having the most beautiful face

Among members of your neighbors' race

As your beloved son you chase.

Beneath The Falter's Lunar Orb

A chorus of crickets composed a concerto

Rising to the mystique of an autumn moon

As the flowing river courses under light

Recalling endless strolls to local diner

For midnight coffee steamingly delicious

While geese prepare for their usual trek

To the southern winter nests while ducks

Guard great integrity of the Holy Temple

Of this city of two municipalities where

Beautiful women wear their summer skirts

For the last time before trees turn nude

And Mexican mothers overwhelmed by crowd

Of children push strollers while sisters

And brothers follow in single file after

Baby carriages with the happy enthusiasm

Of a young puppy off its leash exploring

The terrain of park where people gather.

Going Deeper Into Romantic Autumn

Little Dew drops of female heaven

Sprinkle the city of dreams and desire

Even as short skirts disappear like leaves

From the trees resplendent in fall colors

While hem-lines plunge towards the streets

Like the wind-tossed foliage reminiscent

Of the summer passed onto cooler temps

As lovely angels amble down the foggy avenues

Of male cravings calling out their deep lust

And love taking hold of repressed libidos

Of both men and women scoping cloudy skies

For signs of the coming tranquility of snow

Preparing itself for the frigidity of winter

When all roads will be frozen

And all birds shall have flown

To tropical climes where bikinied beauties

Become beach bunnies beguiling beaus

To be berserk by basis of boyish upbringings.

Sitting On Stoop Of Falter

The day is dark with overcast sky

While clouds hide jets whose roar

Pierce the atmosphere like knives

Like the music of delighted yells

Of children playing on the street

Even as Jesus waits for an advent

Without the trauma of the Rapture

As He sits in sunshine over Earth

Ready to dispense a gift of Grace

Promised by Holy Father in Heaven

Amused greatly at human spectacle

That continues without regard for

The beauty of celestial power and

The Truth of supreme Lord reality

Guiding the course of only sun as

The actions of mankind reflect on

The perfection of a world created

By the eternal wisdom of sole God

Full of love and pity for people.

When Falls The Autumn Rain

.

The lamp of intuition in this solitary room

Is lit by the electricity of longing desire

Which shuts out deep darkness of unrequited

Passion even as taverns are mobbed by girls

Too young to be touched by middle-aged lips

Craving the sweet consummation of relations

Driven by the wish for simple contact while

Geese on the river organize themselves with

Avian instinct for the precise formation of

Their species for their winter migration to

Southern climes where trade-winds blow warm

And sensuous like the smiles of young women

Flush with the first touch of adult-hood as

They sip cocktail with a promiscuous name at

The bar where they drink without conscience

Hoping to find in youthful dreams Casanovas

Who can fulfill their every secret fantasy.

The Last Night Of November

When the full moon careens through the sky
And geese on the river honk and ducks swim
Reluctant to migrate in midst of heat wave
Then does calm reflection of Goddess Diana
Bring beauty of Olympians back to the city
Blessed by Her divine presence illuminated
Through the mirror of the sun by lunar orb
Calling maidens to flash their sensual eye
Into the midnight color of celestial stage
Across which they dance in perfect harmony
To the music of the spheres only they hear
While suitors oblivious drink their liquor
Watching with fervor latest football games
Instead of the loveliness of the ladies in
Curvacious sweaters and spray-on jeans for
The approval of their beaus who don't care
Till after they are too drunk to make-out.

Goddess Of Moon Hunting Maidens

Oh wondrous Diana of perfect form
Your beauty is sublime and divine
And when it's said you are sacred
It is because you are without ego
Self-righteousness or vanity when
Your love for children equals the
Devotion of Jesus to little tykes
While your radiance eclipses fine
Sun whose light defers to you for
Your hours upon this crazy planet
Where you set standard for chaste
Dedication to the ideal of Christ
Who died to infuse life with Love
You exemplify by the sweet melody
Of your voice and insight of mind
With which you dedicate your soul
To the Gospel commandment to seek
God with all your mortal strength
And to love your neighbor totally
Even if they turn into your enemy
For whom you must diligently pray
And truly forgive his trespasses.

Looking For Sole One Love

The consolation of a kiss and the kick of consummation

Drives every person to the void at the edge of passion

Full of longing for the bliss of an ideal relationship

With a lover who knows the secret to marital longevity

Even as we spin on this planet through the stark abyss

Of infinite space too great to conquer in these bodies

Lent to men and women lost from the day of their birth

Celebrated annually while growing into human knowledge

Of the intricacies of this life upon vast Earth sphere

Whereon all comedy and tragedy transpires almost daily

When through the Cosmos words and songs reverberate to

The ears of The Lord seated upon holy celestial throne

With His Son The Word ready to intercede on our behalf

Despite the stains of sin to which everyone is subject

As we seek out the perfect mate to satisfy our amour.

Wondrous Houri Of Holy Vision

Immortal virgin whose radiance of face
Makes bright the sun at dawn with body
Reflecting the constancy of the light of the moon
Make full the Earth with your illuminating beauty
And mesmerize male people with eternal loveliness
Beckoning over deep ocean the ship of pure desire
Even as you stroll through a garden of perfection
Where you alone shall consume the forbidden fruit
Of the knowledge of good and evil as sacred angel
Who flies to ruby throne of holy Paradise calling
Mankind to profound contemplation of an innocence
Made divine through the intervention of your Lord
Who created you to remind planet of hopeful grace
Of salvation to which all humanity openly aspires
Beneath the globe of the celestial constellations
Mirrored in vast infinitude of your longing eyes.

Cravings Of An Old Fart

Alone again at the bar he scopes curvaceous forms
Of fine gals young enough to be his granddaughter
And tries to remember the days when he had access
To busts and bums boobs and buns and a sweet spot
Of insertion even as he longs for casual contacts
He knows shall never occur because he's drug-free
And sober after renouncing the party way long ago
In deep desire to ascertain an essence of reality
That has left him bereft of a loving relationship
Since the youthful days of his Bacchanalian revel
Of intoxication and sexual days he misses greatly
Though proud of his abstinent willpower pondering
A temporary liaison of lustful attraction with an
Amour who could help him overcome his celibacy as
Solitary years still creep by without any respite
From the solitude he cultivates in his messy home
Causing him to fantasize of blissful consummation
Having forgotten actual physical sensation of sex
With female for whom he feels profound affection.

Reflection On The Greatest Craft

The variety of the word order poets string together
Is an approximation of the infinite as every phrase
Has the potential to be a new vein of literary gold
Waiting to be mined by the astute wordsmith seeking
To transform the myopia of reality into work of art
To reveal great beauty and truth seldom found today
When an essence of lovely images is made irrelevant
By the large lack of meaning so many writers desire
To confuse and baffle rather than enlighten readers
Who turn away from the incomprehensible obscurities
With which they are often confronted even as others
Surrender to the void of coherence created by verse
 That say nothing by vast plethora of non sequiturs
Leaving audience thinking about true intelligence.

Ascension Of Blessed Mother Mary

Jesus was already in Heaven when He had to confront

The trauma of maternal mortality after She had watched

Him being beaten sacrificed on the cross and resurrected

Thus justifying the love Lord God felt for Her

But what's a mortal son to do at the sudden demise

Of a divine Mother as he wanders in a surreal fog

Of disbelief and lost hope in his sustaining faith

That all his loved ones would survive until the advent

Of Christ returned to Earth to establish His Kingdom

That is empty without Her whose devotion to Her children

Was forever constant even as Her departure is mourned

As She rises to the realm of angels singing Her name

Through the undying Cosmos perceived from this petty world

Of birth and mirth tears and giggles on which humans live

Praying for a salvation and re-union with adored souls

Who have been born into the higher unknown dimensions

To which every living creature is ultimately consigned

Even as the continuum of reality continues to unfold

With an apathy no longer acceptable in light of the death

Of Her Who is the only eternal sweetheart of Father Judge.

To My Most Beloved Smidge

Confront death with the bold face of God

To deny it victory as you're enfolded in

The embrace of Jesus Who alone knows the

Extent of the suffering you endured when

You spent eighty-plus years on the Earth

Even as you leave for a bit your husband

And your children who shall never forget

Your love devotion compassion and sacred

Understanding before your departure to a

Welcome by your parents and brother gone

To blessed Heaven where the Deity awaits

To give you a vast feeling of true Grace

One cannot know while stuck on the globe

Where you have lived your wonderful life

Full of the joy and happiness you impart

Daily to those in contact with you while

They thank The Lord for pleasure of your

Presence on the globe where all continue

To feel the divine bliss of your history

With which you have always been anointed

As you ascend to celestial banquet table

At which we shall all be one day united.

Things I Must Tell Smidge

Being human I was never the perfect son I wanted to be

But I also never stopped adoring insights of your love

Whose light guided me through darkness of mad sickness

Like a solar candle that did not flicker as I tried to

Remain true to deep mutual unconditional devotion felt

By both of us for the other and my love for sacred you

Has given me the strength to conquer the demons that I

Faced in the hospital as I experienced the totality of

Your dedication to helping me solve my dilemmas as you

Offered me the undying support I needed to overcome my

Problems and I shall treasure you eternally in my soul

Secure in the knowledge our connection lasts always as

I am certain not even death can sever the blessed bond

That'll keep us forever entwined until advent of Jesus

Brings us together at the feast of resurrected Christ.

Nobody Wept Publicly For Smidge

I'm her only son who witnessed demise of Mary

Mother and witnessed grief of devoted husband

The Independent Counsel higher than any judge

Who with me and my sisters Sara and Elizabeth

The pure princesses of the world she has left

Have felt a deep sadness that we cannot cover

As she meets holy God at mansion He has built

For family she so loved for eighty-four years

Though we have shed no tears at her leaving I

Feel in my heart and spirit while days follow

One another in a progression that must change

Without the security of her loving compassion

To shield us from sun rays of indifference we

Encounter now she is no more presence in time

Or space in which all earthly creatures exist

Even as my soul longs to cry at her departure

That creates a vast void in fabric of planets

Of solar system empty of the passion we crave

While awaiting our own predestined mortality.

Dale Remembering Mother Of All

This is poem about Mother Mary

Who for four score did tarry

And mantle of divinity did carry

Through times both joyful and scary

In years that made many wary

Though never becoming with life teary

Until in ground we did bury

Her sacred body tired but merry

As to Heaven she caught ferry

Transporting her to Feast of Lord

As from this planet she soared

Attached to the holy umbilical cord

Which into her soul enthusiasm poured

Because she refused to be bored

And treasures with God she stored

While her family she truly adored

Even as her pain she ignored

When all the angelic trumpets roared.

Unable To Believe She's Gone

To her husband she expressed the essence of sensuality

While to her children her beauty defined her sweetness

As she journeyed through this world full of compassion

And devotion to those lucky enough to experience amour

She always exuded from the moment of her blessed birth

To the second she passed into the next realm where she

Will impress all who are seated at the Feast of Christ

With her celestial sophistication reunited with family

Of her youth who preceded her past the Gates of Heaven

And the void on Earth she leaves at her last departure

Cannot be filled by the scope of billions of millennia

Of light years stretching across the Cosmos even while

The significance of her demise cannot be calculated as

Those who are left behind fight to find the meaning of

Her flight into the graceful arms of Jesus she forever

Adored in the profane machinations of this human home.

Composing In Darkness Of Candle

The lights across the courtyard taunt me

With their constancy of illumination

Surviving sixth day of after-storm blackout

Trying to will electricity to return

While utility crews work through the night

But I'm safe in the sanctuary of this room

Tired of curfews cold showers and no coffee

Which are petty complaints compared to devastation

To properties destroyed in newspaper pictures

For which necessities are now impossible luxuries

Even as many thank Lord for escaping with their lives

Despite the destruction that touches millions

Who have lost their homes and assumed sense of security

To the wrath of Nature let loose on great city

That has never experienced such stormy violence

In the last century more powerful than public

Could possibly conceive in their worst nightmares

As the hidden sun rises over a transformed world

From which there is no simple awakening.

Not To Dabble In Metaphysics

In this room the chosen spot where I will spend eternity

Where a thousand million billion trillion years

Is but a nanosecond in a forever of which no human

Can truly conceive and can I devote my heart to a woman

For such an epoch when every morning brings to light

A finer female beauty to the streets of this holy city

Isolated like the clouds of New Jerusalem hovering

Unseen in anticipation of the return of our Lord

To signal the end of tragedy but not Earthly days

While mankind lives in an oblivious present in which to see

The Reality of inevitable mortality as Infinity

Is beyond the capacity to comprehend spinning around the sun

That one day will send its final warmth to this world

Before it implodes like the Universe at its outer limits

Of expansion and all space and time will re-converge

To a single particle of matter waiting to explode with violence

To recommence the endless scenario of the Deity Who rules

Over the Omniverse humanity can hypothesize as actual in theory

But cannot demonstrate as true while every moment brings

A new child of unlimited potential to the ephemeral globe

The majority assumes will always remain the same.

Dale Hits DEW Year Writing

Tonight my Spaceship left the atmosphere

On a chill evening perfectly clear

From its position in upper stratosphere

But I didn't have a beer

To celebrate advent of another year

Because the Apocalypse is very near

Which I face with little fear

And Chuckie will The Dialina steer

Through the void vast and sheer

Leaving me nothing in his will

Whom cancer like many did kill

Overcoming stigma of being mentally ill

For he daily took his pill

So many women love him still

To whom he gave a thrill

Putting them through his drinking drill

As many mugs he did fill

And consumed with a considerable skill.

Thirty-Seven Years In Hackensack

I must begin to rebuild the domicile of my self

Without the rock foundation of dear Mother Mary

For whose demise I've mourned but not tearfully

Grieved recalling her happy compassion and love

And still there are barmates with whom I cannot

Enjoy a brew being sober while remembering hour

Of arrival in The Holy City where I've spent my

Entire adult life and conquered various spirits

Who sought to make me psychotic as I partied on

Substances that drove me nuts though being glad

When sanity reappeared after eight years and an

Innate peace came over me as my personality was

Transformed into that of nice person I am today

Who lives by regimen of medications and therapy

Ready to pursue an immortal existence if Christ

Returns to the Earth with Smidge and many other

Friends who already ascended to blissful Heaven

As good souls who will rule with divine justice

And will I pray find me innocent of myriad sins

Committed when I was mad with a mental illness.

Last Dale Before Mayan Armageddon

It was lust at first sight

When she entered bar that night

Her smile source of celestial light

While being of stature somewhat slight

Although she was of acceptable height

Her rainbow aura being very bright

Before she had a major fight

With boyfriend over what was right

Which caused her to become uptight

But she is forever Queen Muse

Though other lovers she did choose

Making to Puerto Rico permanent cruise

Where she enjoys the ocean views

And tries to avoid evening news

Which cause good people serious blues

Watching innocent victims pay their dues

As cops for evil perpetrators peruse

And righteous pray at local pews.

Heart Dale For Queen Muse

Would you be my only Valentine

You with lovely heart so fine

To whom my devotion I assign

Who makes my lonely spirit shine

As delicate as rare vintage wine

Always hoping to make you mine

Being most inspirational Muse of nine

Causing me for you to pine

While into reveries I happily recline

For it's you I truly adore

Far from room of my amour

When you lie on tropical shore

As you touch my hearty core

Where my desirous feelings I store

Which reflect the thunder of Thor

When into my thoughts you soar

It's you I ask God for

Seeking forever to please you more.

Heart Dale For Olympian Diana

You're secret desire of normal men

Guardian angel of every pure maiden

Who is innocent of carnal sin

Unlike Eve expelled from perfect Garden

She found herself with Adam in

When epoch of man did begin

For Paradise they did not win

Before they had any human kin

While devil lost his evil grin

But even if not a Goddess

I know you are a Princess

In line to become holy Highness

Who shall enjoy a great success

Creating always more love not less

By performing rites of sacred Priestess

Until you inherit mantle of Empress

Leading mankind to fix worldly mess

With beautiful mind and golden tress.

A Sonnet For Mystery Valentine

Sweet Melina you are so beautiful

To you I shall always be dutiful

For I know you are a Dietess Greek

Whose grandiosity makes my heart weak

Though we have been friends for a score of years

Keeping in contact only by the phone

But we have never caused each other tears

Despite reality we're both alone

But you've inherited crown of Duck Queen

Through essence of your lovely and pure soul

Growing with grace into your royal role

The most regal woman I've ever seen

Who inspires me to pursue written art

Perhaps it's time for our Romance to start.

Birthday Sonnet For Purest Sweetheart

Most beloved and greatly desired Jill

The torch I carry for you burns bright still

As I remember exploits on campus

Which I tried to turn into a circus

So you would be eternally amused

By variety of pleasures found there

Making sure that you were never abused

Wanting to run my fingers through your hair

While we exchanged a long sensual kiss

And I have not seen you in twenty years

Living in room across the street from Sears

Lacking only you to complete my bliss

And on this special day I send my love

Praying we'll unite in fine Heaven above.

Sonnet To Only Queen Muse

Let's dance together across cosmic floor
Since I want forever to be your boy
For you are lovely as Helen of Troy
While being saintly pure at inner core
As you seek to be worthy of Christ's Grace
And accept your lot among human race
In which you shine bright as a nova star
Whose light is seen by people near and far
But I've fallen for your matchless beauty
And the perfection of your female form
Which to defend is now my truthful duty
As we weather the Apocalyptic storm
Where you exemplify meaning of love
And shan't become sacrificial dove.

I Cannot Stop Desiring You

I search for an ideal in a fractured world

A woman perfect for me despite human flaws

And amour between male and female can't be

Without a healthy dose of romantic lust as

Consummation is real goal of all relations

And I want to caress your luscious breasts

And kiss ravenously your whole divine body

But instead I sit alone in this petty room

Dreaming of locking lips in a hard embrace

And feeling the shiver of your soul giggle

In my desirous arms energizing the longing

Of my heart though you refuse all advances

Leaving me with burning spirit unfulfilled

For I have never loved a woman as I do you

For as long as the years I count endlessly

Hoping one day you will awake in deep love

With me even as I consider the obstacles I

Know prevent you from devoting yourself to

The life-long bachelor I shall forever be.

The Woman From Secret Dreams

Oh most lovely and gracious Nicole
Who's to someone mate of soul
What exactly is your special role
In design to make reality whole
For you are gorgeous and droll
And cause chapel bells to toll
Since making you Bride is goal
With diamond ring come from coal
Despite hoping Cowboys win Super Bowl
As your beauty brings a smile
To all who appreciate feminine style
Whose number suitors love to dial
Walking for you that extra mile
They pray leads to wedding aisle
While smart phone comments you file
When male libidos you innocently rile
After getting to know you awhile
Regal as Cleopatra of the Nile.

The Current State Of Dale

For five years I have shown

I can prosper without a bone

Because Lord gives bodies on loan

Communing with Jesus on celestial throne

Before Whom I lay myself prone

While I wait by the phone

Hearing nothing but the dial tone

Praying I shan't be forever alone

As poetic skills I dutifully hone

Trying with verse to create sense

Out of dark chaotic present tense

With imagery I dare not mince

In poems many claim are dense

To be read a millennium hence

When critics can't make me wince

Written for enjoyment of Christ Prince

And absolute lover not known since

Intoxication became for me major offense.

Velvet Ultimately Married Someone Else

I remember the slim delicacy of her long fingers

And the nuanced fragility of her radiant smile

And the Trilogy of fantasy novels she inspired me to write

In which she is the supernaturally magical heroine

And the rides she gave me every morning to school

And my fear of telling her the depths of my devotion

Even as we lost hours to intimate phone conversations

For she was the most beautiful redhead I ever saw

With a head of hair reminiscent of the scarlet dawn

But my reticence kept me from realizing actual Romance

As we graduated without any declarations of love

So she became a glamorous airline stewardess

And fell for a pilot

Who could give her everything I as a poet I could not afford

And thus my memories of her exuberance and loveliness

Are the sole souvenirs I retain from the four years

We passed together in pursuit of our mutual dreams

And sometimes my heart longs for the bliss she induced

As I write poems in an effort to capture elusive amour

That seems slipping away with each passing birthday over fifty

Though I thank Lord she is happy with her children

And husband even when I ponder possibilities I missed

To make her my dedicated Bride before she was introduced

To the man who would finally win her wondrous heart.

Erisian Festival Come And Gone

It was a cloudy night three millennia ago

When Great Goddess looked down through the spectrum

Of a full rainbow halo of her lunacy to underworld

Of Hades where sat Achilles on his discontented throne

Wanting another chance at life on Earth far from dead

Over whom he ruled in silent frustration and decided

This was the human male to whom She would give her heart

And so caused him to be reborn in this anachronistic age

Even as She plotted Her maneuvers to reach this planet

Long after the rest of the Olympians had progressed

Into disembodied spirit seeking a new universal home

Leaving control of the world to Her Who was of all

The Fairest obsessed by Her ideal of warrior Romance

As She stalked Her beloved in the shadow of The Lord

Who overwhelmed Her divine compatriots with vast powers

Even Zeus could not conceive as She pursued Her desire

To put away Her divinity and dedicate Herself to a life

Of domestic bliss leaving behind the discord of Her past

While Achilles took care of the battles of amour created

By their mutual devotion to the other until they both

Ascended to the thrones left empty by the deities

Of the ancient reality from which they had grown strong

Together from the instant of their very first embrace.

When This Life Is Over

I imagine myself laid in fresh grave

And mourning friends and kin over me weep

As they remember gifts to world I gave

Before sinking into a restless sleep

Where I listen to sounds I cannot hear

Although the voices are distinct and clear

But I cannot pronounce soft words I speak

Overwhelmed by stench of cadaver reek

Thus never again to feel drop of rain

Or no more to enjoy succulent taste

Of pasta covered by tomato paste

In the underworld where there is no pain

After I leave behind this lonely place

Setting soul free to soar through time and space.

When I Consider Final Judgment

I cannot conceive of myself dying

To be sentenced to an eternal grave

In cold coffin six feet under lying

Becoming in afterlife Satan's slave

While hoping to rise to mansion of Lord

To where Christ after Easter humbly soared

To claim His seat on the Heavenly throne

From whence light of His salvation has shone

Even as I reflect on state of death

Convinced it is a false reality

For I believe in immortality

After I exhale my last earthly breath

Since I have faith in truth of holy Grace

Which is fact for the entire human race.

In Celebration Of Christmas Season

Let us worship the anointed baby

Who represents all humanity may be

Blessed in His sacred Father's sight

Who brought into world salvation's light

Lying content in a humble manger

Born into life of mortal danger

For Earthly father Joseph was wary

About virgin he vowed to marry

Not knowing how Bride became mother

Without ever having laid with another

But by Holy Spirit she conceived

So the planet its savior received

His birth announced by angels divine

Who told shepherds all was fine

As they searched for celestial sign

Until guiding star rose in east

Stopping over Jesus protected by beast

In barn where He never wept

While Magi for Him vigil kept

Giving Him treasured gifts of love

When Christ left heavenly throne above.

Reflections After Delicious Christmas Dinner

The reason people think I'm deep

Is because most people are asleep

Unaware we live in collective dream

Where milk separates from the cream

As majority of humans seek wealth

At expense of their mental health

Not bothering to avoid psychic sickness

Which takes hold with horrid quickness

While too few attempt to find

A perfect serenity of the mind

Apathetic to what is left behind

Searching for true salvation to discover

Secret bliss of an ideal lover

Out of whose arms grows amour

Steady as waves upon sandy shore

At the edge of vast ocean

From which emerges the peculiar notion

That real passion can be bound

By the soft and familiar sound

Of a sweet beloved's liquid voice

Rising above the planet's endless noise.

When I Am Finally Gone

I will dwell in the house of The Lord
Who arose and to a divine home soared
For He brought to humans sacred Grace
As by His blood He blessed whole race
Of sinners whom He taught how to pray
So it became possible for folk to say
That all men were the children of God
Learning His ways in an ephemeral bod
We are lent from hour of infant birth
Until it's time for us to quit Earth.

About The Poet

D.E.Walsh has been dedicated to the Poetic Craft since his graduation from Fairleigh Dickinson University (Teaneck-Hackensack Campus) in 1985. An alumnus of Phillips Exeter Academy, he has spent his entire adult life in Hackensack, to where he came quite by chance in 1976 at the age of twenty. He has written six novels and at least 1500 poems in his literary career. His current project is an autobiography telling of his adventures before and after his arrival in New Jersey. He is a life-long bachelor still looking for the right woman to be his Bride.

An Explanation Of The Different Forms

I have always been fascinated by new poetic forms. This collection is founded on some forms I have developed (and named) myself, among them:

The Box: Where every line has the same number of characters. These include "Dewey Boxes" (ten lines apiece); "Dewey Genius Boxes" (a couplet-rhymed Dewey Box); and a modified Box (the line length has more than one length in a successive order);

The Dale: Six words a line with two sets of nine rhymes apiece;

Open: No rule for its rhyme, meter, or words per line;

Roxette: Six words for 21 lines with 9 rhyming couplets and a triplet;

DEW Sonnet: 14 lines but every quatrain has a different rhyme scheme with a closing couplet.

People ask me how I produce with such rigid forms and I tell them "I honestly don't know" without violating either form or content. But they seem to work.

www.ingramcontent.com/pod-product-compliance
Lightning Source LLC
Chambersburg PA
CBHW070528030426
42337CB00016B/2160

* 9 7 8 0 6 1 5 8 3 4 9 2 4 *